BRUCE GERBARG

Library of Congress Catalog Card Number: 55-10549

RIGHT AND WRONG

BY DOROTHY K. KRIPKE · PICTURES BY BOBRI

BEHRMAN HOUSE, INC. · PUBLISHERS · NEW YORK

In LET'S TALK ABOUT RIGHT AND WRONG, I have tried, within the comprehension and experience limitations of a child, to present a traditional system of ethics. This is but a beginning. The imaginative parent or teacher can do much to supplement the text by adding ideas and multiplying examples.

There are some aspects of the good life which I have not touched upon because they are, to my mind, beyond the child's grasp or beyond his experience and interest. These are better left for the more mature mind. Freedom of will, e.g., is constantly stated but never discussed or analysed. Reward and punishment are not treated except in the constant emphasis that virtue is its own reward. The problem of evil in the world is touched only lightly. At this age it is futile to explore fully so difficult a theological and philosophical problem.

My approach to the subject of the good life is a religious one. From the belief in One God and the concept of imitatio dei, *there develops a clear and consistent ethical code. Thus the compelling reason for honesty is not that "it pays," but rather that it ennobles man and expresses the divine spark in him. And dishonesty is wrong, not because "it doesn't pay," but rather because it causes man to degenerate, reduces the divine image, and brings man closer to the brute.*

Because I feel that childhood is the best time to start teaching an ethical approach to life (and no age is too young!), I have tried to treat the subject on a child's level. The task, to be sure, was not an easy one, but it seemed to be well worth the undertaking. I hope the result meets the need.

D.K.K.

Omaha, Nebr.

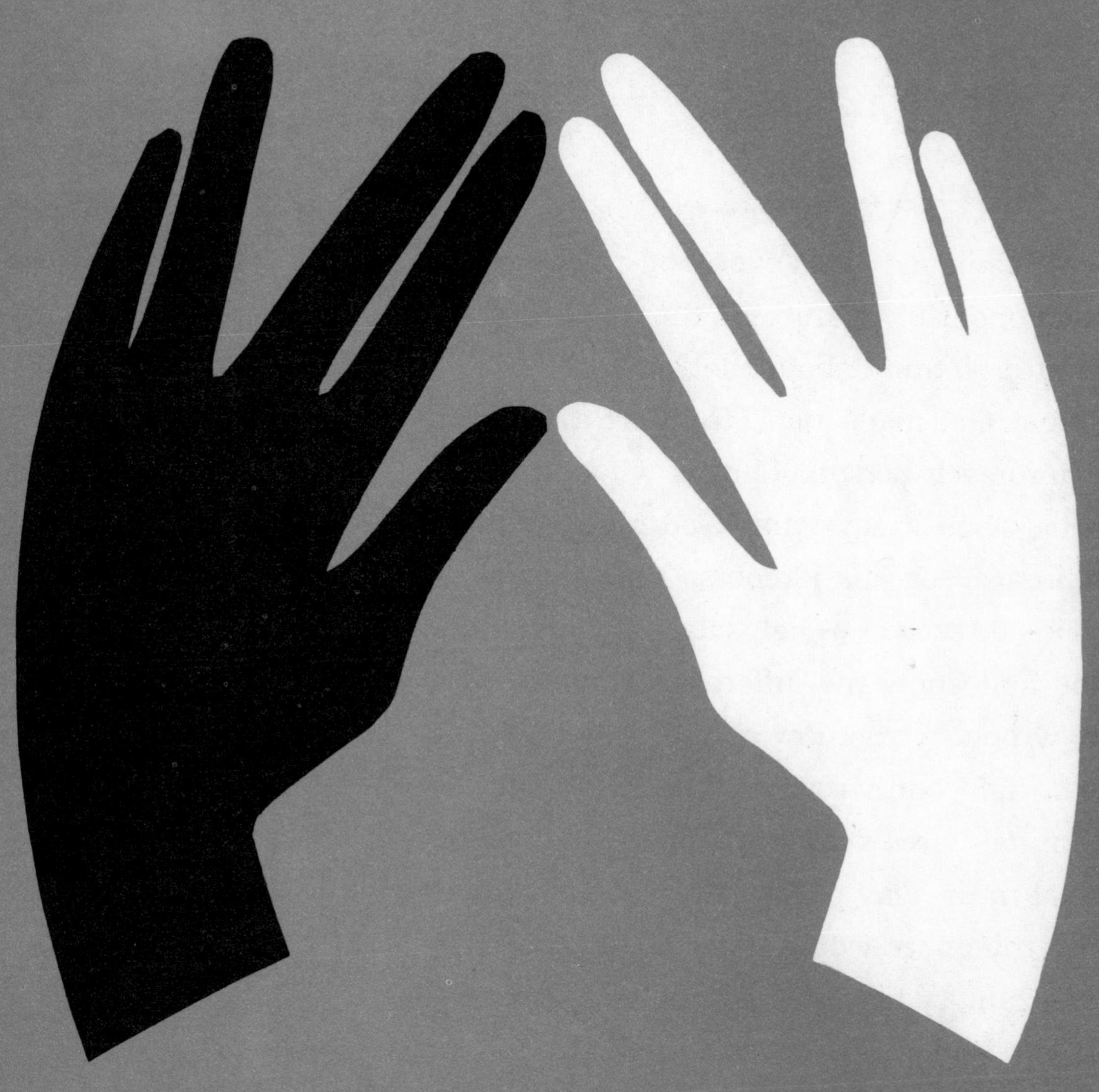

This book is dedicated
to Goldie Karp, my Mother, who helped me learn right from wrong,
and to Saul, Madeline, and Netta, whom I have tried to teach....

People are so wonderful
And special in God's sight
Because they know the difference
Between what's wrong and right.

People—you and I and everybody else—are the most wonderful creatures in the world. Did you ever stop to think about that?

When God made man, He put a little of Himself into each person. That is what the Bible means when it says that God made man "in His image," or His likeness. This tiny bit of God inside each of us helps us learn and understand and know the difference between right and wrong. And knowing the difference between right and wrong makes us special.

Animals are wonderful, but they are not special in the way people are special. They do many things we would not do. Have you ever seen a hungry pig poking about in garbage to find his dinner? He doesn't mind the mess a bit. That's all right for a pig, but it is not all right for people. You and I like fresh food served on a clean table. We like it to be pretty, all yellow and golden brown and green and red. We are different from animals.

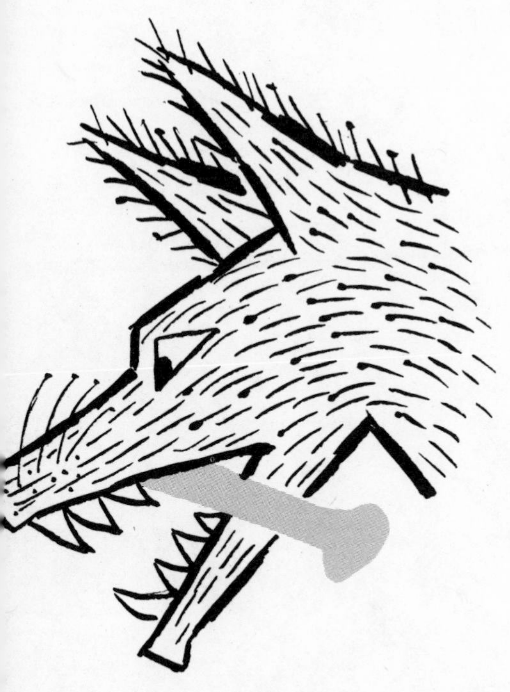

There is a more important difference between people and animals. Animals don't know the difference between right and wrong. A big dog will grab a bone away from a puppy. He doesn't even know he is doing something wrong. But you and I don't grab what belongs to someone else, even if the other person is smaller than we are. We know the difference between right and wrong. A mouse will squeeze and wriggle his way into a house and eat whatever food he likes. He doesn't even know that he is stealing or that stealing is wrong. That is all right for a mouse, but not for people. You and I don't take things that belong to others.

People are different from animals. People know the difference between right and wrong. When we do something wrong, we usually know it is wrong. Then we are less wonderful, and we feel less special. But when we do what is right, we feel warm and satisfied and comfortable inside. The tiny bit of God inside us that tells us what is right makes us feel wonderful and special. When we are special, we are less like the animals and more like God.

We all can be God's partners
And build a world that's good,
If we but choose to do what's right.
Now don't you think we should?

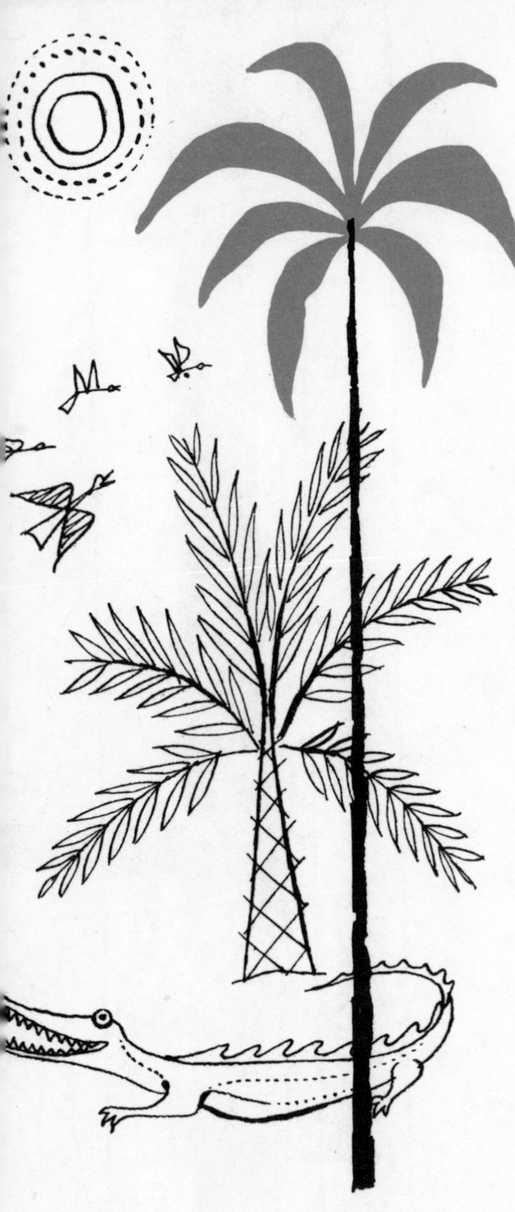

Long ago, when God made the world and people to live in it, He said, "People will be My partners. They will help make the world better and better. People are able to think, and to know what is right and what is wrong. They can choose between bad and good, between wrong and right. When they choose the right way to live, they help make themselves and the world better." If they choose to, people can be partners of God.

Animals cannot make our world better. But people can. When birds feel the cold breath of winter in the air, they fly to warmer lands. When bears feel the crisp, tingly cold, they find a comfortable place and go to sleep for the winter. But people, long ago, found better ways to keep warm. They made warmer clothes. They built strong, sturdy homes. They learned how to make fire. They found different ways to heat their homes. People found ways to make the world better.

People found many other ways to make the world more comfortable. They built smooth-sailing ships and fast-moving trains and swift automobiles and high-flying planes to take us quickly and pleasantly from one place to another. They invented many machines to make our work easier. They found wonderful medicines to make us well or to keep us from getting sick. People are still finding ways to make the world more comfortable and more healthful.

People can think and speak and tell each other things. People can learn from each other. We can learn even from people who lived long, long ago, by reading the books they wrote. The more we learn and the more we know, the more we can do. When people share their ideas and work together, they can do wonderful things. And because people can think and learn and understand, they can make themselves better too. They can try to be more fair and kind, more honest and loving. When people are better, they help make the world better. Then they are really God's helpers.

You and I need not invent something new to help the world—although some of you probably will some day! What we all can do is choose wisely between right and wrong. When we do something wrong or bad, we do not help. Then we are not being God's partners. But every time we do the right thing, we *do* help. Then we are pleased with ourselves. It feels very good to be God's helper.

Would you like to know more about right and wrong, and just how you and I can be God's partners? Then let us think about it together.

We all can make a better world
If we will love each other
And treat each person everywhere
As though he were a brother.

The world is full of millions of people—really more than two billion. And all of them are very much like you and me. They are happy sometimes, and sad other times. They can be frightened or brave or worried. They get hungry or thirsty or tired or sleepy just as we do. They are hurt just as easily as we are. And they can have just as much fun as we can.

God, who made you and me, made all of them too. God put a little of Himself into all of them too. He made them different from animals. He made them special, just like us. He loves all of them just as He loves us.

All people, everywhere, are very important to God. They may have different colored hair or eyes or skin, but that doesn't matter. When you and I paint a picture, we may have favorite colors—red or blue or yellow or green. But when God made people, He had no favorite colors. All people are equally important to God.

All people, whether they are beautiful or ugly or weak or strong, are important to God. The shortest child and the tallest, the fattest and the skinniest, are all important to God.

Even if they wear peculiar clothes or eat strange foods, other people are still just as important to God. Our clothes and foods seem strange to them too! Yet we are all equally important to God.

Whether they are rich or poor, whether they live in beautiful big houses or tiny huts, whether they live in princely palaces or in tumble-down shacks, all people are equally important to God.

You are as important to God, to your parents, and to yourself as all the whole world. And every other person is just that important too.

If we want to be really special and partners with God, then we must always remember that other people—all people—are just as important as we are. We must show by the way we treat them that we know how important they are. We must love them as we love ourselves. This is what we mean when we talk about "brotherhood." God loves all the people in the world. We can be God's partners and help make the world better if we love all people too.

Other people have their rights,
And so, of course, have we.
If all of us were always fair,
How good the world would be!

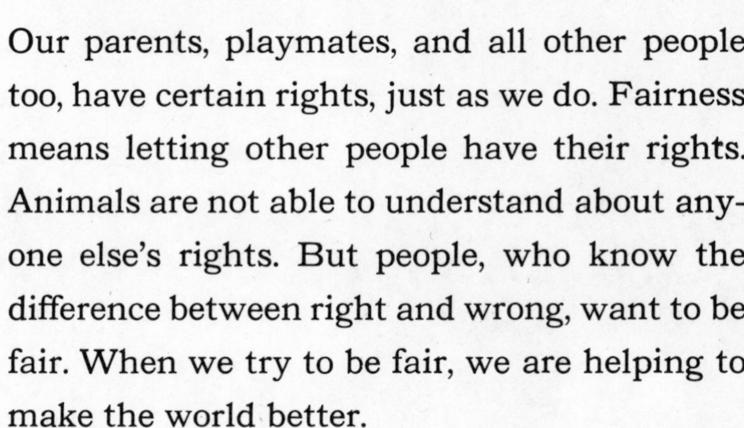

Our parents, playmates, and all other people too, have certain rights, just as we do. Fairness means letting other people have their rights. Animals are not able to understand about anyone else's rights. But people, who know the difference between right and wrong, want to be fair. When we try to be fair, we are helping to make the world better.

We all know about playing fair in a game. It is not fair to peek under the blindfold when we are "pinning the tail on the donkey." If we do not play fair, it does not make us feel good to win the game. Even if we win, the little bit of God inside us is disappointed if we have done something wrong. If we play fair, we feel comfortable inside ourselves whether we win or lose.

Being fair is important not only in games, but in everything we think or say or do at home, in school, and everywhere else. If your friend listens to phonograph records with you, it is fair to take turns in choosing the records. In school it is fair for each child to have a turn at things that are fun—like writing on the blackboard. And it is only fair for every child in the class to do his share in keeping the classroom clean and neat.

In a family, too, we must be fair and remember each other's rights. It is only fair for you to come to dinner when you are called. At the table, it is not fair for one person to do all the talking. It is fair for everyone, children and grown-ups alike, to have a turn. And after the meal, it is only fair for you to do whatever you can to help clean up.

You have a right to play with your toys. That's what they are for, isn't it? But it is only fair for you to pick them up and put them away neatly when you are through playing. In a family *all* the people should be fair with each other. And, of course, we should be fair with *all* people, even those who are not part of our family. This is what we mean when we talk about "justice."

When we remember other people's rights, and are fair, we help make the world better. Then we are God's partners.

God is kind and merciful,
And we should be kind too,
Helpful, thoughtful, friendly,
In all we say and do.

God made all the people—and other creatures—in the world. He loves all the creatures He made. And He treats them all with kindness and mercy. If we too love God's creatures, people and other living things, then we are a little like God. If we too treat them with kindness and mercy, then we are God's helpers.

Kindness means being thoughtful and helpful and friendly. When we are kind, we show our love for the creatures God made. That is why kindness is also called "*loving*-kindness."

It is kind to help a lady with the cans and packages that have dropped from her grocery bag. It is kind to help a little boy look for the dime he has lost. When we are helpful, we are being kind.

It is kind to be thoughtful. It is thoughtful not to tell your friend that his brand-new puppet is not so fine as yours. It is thoughtful to share some of the treats you get at a birthday party with your sister or brother. When you are thoughtful you show people that you love them.

Sometimes we can be kind by just a friendly look or touch. A warm smile, a hug, a touch, all seem to say, "I love you so much that I want to help you." And just saying that, in a smile or touch, seems to help a great deal. It makes us feel better to know that people want to help us.

Mercy means being kind even when the person we are being kind to doesn't exactly deserve it. Suppose you are walking happily along the street. A big boy comes up to you and pushes and shoves you for no reason at all. Then he walks on. Suddenly he slips on some wet leaves. His books and papers and pencils tumble to the sidewalk. Some coins bounce out of his pocket. And there he is, stretched out on the walk. Just then he really has less right than usual to expect your help. If you are kind enough to help him get up and pick up his things, then you are being merciful. Mercy means helping people when they have less right than usual to expect kindness.

People—you and I—should be kind and merciful not only to other people, but also to animals and all other living things. It is not kind to take an egg out of a bird's nest, or to tease a puppy with food you don't intend to give him. It *is* kind to throw crumbs of bread outdoors for the birds in the winter. Loving-kindness and mercy are the way we show our love for *all* God's creatures.

God is kind and merciful to all living things. If we want to be special and more like God, if we want to be God's helpers, we should be kind and merciful too.

It's right and good and fair
That all of us should share
Our fun and food and toys
With other girls and boys.

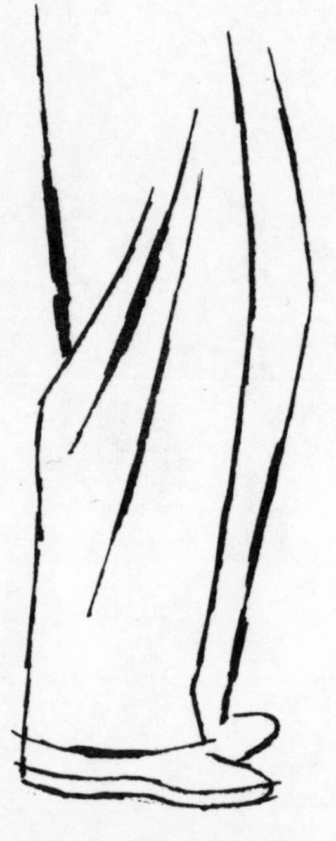

It is good to give, and it is good to share. When we share the things we have, we make the world better, and we are more like God.

God gives us many good things. He made us in a wonderful way. People are the only creatures that can stand up straight. We can run and swim and do all sorts of things. We can smell the sweetness of a red, red rose. We can taste the delicious flavor of a ripe, juicy, golden peach. We can see and enjoy the cool, smooth beauty of pure white snow. We can feel the furry softness of a warm little kitten. God gives us wonderful bodies. He gives us food to make our bodies strong. He gives us minds with which we can think and learn and make plans. He gives us speech, so that we can tell other people what we think. And He gives us many other good things. Everything is given to us by God.

It is only fair and right that we share with other people some of the things God has given us. We can share our toys and treats with other children. We can share our fun and our ideas. And we can give food to people who are hungry. We can give money to poor people to help them buy the food or clothing or medicines they need.

Sometimes we don't know any people who need help. But synagogues and temples and churches collect money for the poor. And other groups of people, too, like the Community Chest, collect money to help those who need help. If we share some of our money, then we are helping other people, and we are helping to make the world better.

If we are selfish and say, "I have just enough for myself and none to spare," then we are choosing the wrong thing. But if we share what we have, then we are a little more like God. God gives us all so much. When we give, we are really God's partners.

When we share with our families and friends —whom we know and like—we are very good. When we share with people we don't even know—like people in faraway lands—we are even better. When we share with people and help them and teach them and make it possible for them to take care of themselves, then we are best of all. All people who share what God has given them are making the world better. They are God's partners.

In all we do
And all we say,
At home or school,
At work or play,
The way to live
Is the honest way.

The Ten Commandments tell us "Thou shalt not steal" and "Thou shalt not bear false witness." This means that stealing and lying are wrong, and being honest is right. Honesty is one way we have of showing that we are special and different from animals, that we are more like God.

A child, or a grown-up, who is not honest, who steals or cheats or lies, almost always gets into trouble. He may be caught and punished. Even if he is not punished when he is caught, the sad look in his mother's eyes or the disappointed look on the face of his father, or teacher, or friend, is punishment enough. But if he is *not* caught, what happens then? Sometimes it is even worse than being caught. He worries about being found out. If his mother looks at him, he wonders, "Does she know?" If his father calls him, he is sure that Dad knows. And the worry and unhappiness go on—and on—and on.

The stolen penny seems to burn a hole in his pocket. The lie seems to burn a hot, worried, sick feeling deep inside him. The little bit of God inside him tells him how wrong he was. When we lie or cheat or steal, we are less like God.

When we are not honest, we are less special. Then we are more like animals and less like God. A fox will steal a chicken, and a squirrel will steal nuts. We can't blame the fox and the squirrel for stealing, because animals don't know the difference between right and wrong. But we know the difference, and we can choose between right and wrong. When we choose to do wrong, to lie or cheat or steal, we are more like animals. When we choose to be honest and truthful, we are more like God.

If everybody were honest, just think how much better the world would be! We can help make the world better by being honest. When we are honest, we are God's partners.

No person has the right to say,
"I'm better than the rest."
For all of us are wonderful,
But none of us is best.

Each one of us is as important as the whole world!

You and I—and every other person—are very wonderful. We are more wonderful than the strongest lion or the prettiest peacock or the biggest elephant or the fastest deer. We have a little of God in us.

Because we are so wonderful and important, it is right for us to take good care of ourselves. We must keep ourselves as clean and healthy as we can. We must learn as much as we can. We must always try to choose the right thing to do. We must always try to remember that we are a little like God.

But we must always remember that every other person is a little like God too. Every other person is important and wonderful too.

And we must remember that no one of us is perfect. Each of us—even the best of us—does the wrong thing sometimes. And even the worst of us does the right thing sometimes. No one of us is perfect. Only God is perfect.

No one of us can do everything. Perhaps you have a beautiful voice and can sing at parties. But can you paint a lovely picture? One child can run very fast. Another is especially bright and can learn quickly. Still another can make interesting things with clay. And still another may be prettier or stronger. No one of us is perfect, and no one of us can do everything. Nor should we expect to be able to do everything. For only God is perfect. Only God can do everything.

It is very strange that the more we do and the more we know, the more we realize how much we cannot do and do not know. The greater we are and the better we are, the more we realize our littleness in the world.

When we remember both our importance and our littleness in the world, we know our true value. Then we cannot be "stuck-up" or "put on airs" or boast or brag about ourselves. Wonderful as we are, we are not perfect. We cannot do everything, and we are not more important than other people. It is wrong to act or feel as though we were more important. It is right to remember that *all* people are very important and very little at the same time—and so are you and I.

We should be truly sorry
For any wrong we do,
And just as God forgives us, we
Should be forgiving, too.

God is perfect, but *we* are not—not one of us. We all make mistakes, and we all do the wrong thing at times.

We are not *always* fair.

We are not *always* honest.

We are not *always* kind.

We do not *always* share.

We do not *always* remember our littleness in the world.

We do not *always* do what is right.

People cannot be perfect. But we can always try to be *better* than we have been. We can (and should) be sorry if we have done something wrong. If we are really and honestly sorry, then we try to do something about it. We say, "I'm sorry," and that helps quite a bit. Then the person we have hurt feels better, and we feel a little better too. But usually we can do more than just say we are sorry. If we have taken something that belongs to someone else, we can return it. If we are really sorry and really try to do better, then we have learned even from doing wrong.

When we are really sorry and really try to do better, then people almost always forgive us. If we are sorry, our parents forgive us because they love us. They know that no one is perfect. And God forgives us because He loves us. He knows that people cannot be perfect. People can only try to be better.

If we want to be a little like God, then we too must forgive other people. Suppose your friend, by accident or even in a burst of temper, tore your book or broke your toy. If he is truly sorry and says so, and offers to save his pennies until he can buy you another, you forgive him. And when you see how very sorry he really is, you probably tell him not to worry about it. His being sorry makes *him* a better person, and it makes you feel better. Your forgiveness makes *you* a better person, and it makes him feel better. When we forgive, we are a little more like God.

We should respect our parents,
And all our teachers, too,
And show them love and honor them
Because it is their due.

From the time you were a tiny baby, your parents have tried to help you and teach you. They have done this gladly, and they always will, because they love you so much. You love them, too, even though you cannot help them quite so much as they help you. But there are other ways that you *can* show them your love. You can respect them and honor them and listen to them.

When you were little, Mother said, "Don't touch that knife," because she didn't want you to cut yourself. Father said, "No matches," because he didn't want you to burn yourself. When Mother says, "Not too many sweets" or Father says, "Do your schoolwork," they are still trying to help you.

Honoring our parents means many things. When we are very young, it means obeying. The baby who has just learned to walk is much safer if she obeys her parents and does not wander across the street. When we are a little older, honoring our parents means listening to them and learning from them. Then we want to know *why* we may not stay up late every night, or *why* we should brush our teeth. If we ask our parents, they will usually give us good reasons. When we are still older, honoring our parents means talking things over with them and telling them what we think and why we think it. And at the same time, it means listening to what they think too.

As we grow older we learn to think for ourselves more and more. Wise parents help us to grow up and to think for ourselves. They help us learn to decide for ourselves what is right and what is wrong.

When we talk things over with our parents and teachers, we are usually helping ourselves. And at the same time, we are saying, "I care for you and trust you and love you." When we show our parents that we care for them and love them, we are obeying one of the Ten Commandments, the one that tells us, "Honor your father and your mother."

Our bodies and our minds can give
Us much of joy and pleasure,
If we use them wisely as
A very precious treasure.

Life is a very precious gift from God. It is right to enjoy life. God wants us to enjoy life, and He wants us to enjoy the world into which He put us. When we remember how special we are, when we choose the right thing to do, then we feel satisfied inside ourselves. When we feel good inside, life is better for us.

There are some things in life we do not enjoy. Sometimes we have pain. Sometimes we have troubles, like missing a party because of the mumps. And sometimes we have bigger troubles that hurt us even more. No one can really understand all about the troubles in the world. But we do know that being brave helps. Remembering that God knows what He is doing helps us to be brave, even if we do not understand. And being brave helps us when we have pain or trouble.

There are many things in life that we can, and should, enjoy. We enjoy our bodies when we run and swim and skip and dance. We enjoy the food that makes our bodies strong. We enjoy a drink of cool clear water, and we are refreshed by a tall glass of white milk. We enjoy the good smell of a cake baking in the oven. We enjoy the coolness of crisp white sheets and the warm coziness of soft, woolly blankets. We are able to enjoy our bodies, and our bodies help us to enjoy the world around us.

We can, and should, enjoy other people. It is fun to play and talk and be with our friends. We enjoy our families, our parents and sisters and brothers and other relatives. We enjoy getting married and having a husband or a wife to share life with when we grow up. When we are married, it is very good to have children. We enjoy our children very much.

We can enjoy our minds too. It's fun to study and learn about the world. Understanding things about the world helps us to enjoy it more. Ants and bees are much more interesting to us if we know how they build their own little worlds. There is wonderful pleasure in learning and knowing and understanding.

Learning also helps us to know the difference between right and wrong. As we learn more, we become a little more like God. The more we know, the more we realize how special we are. Then we are better able to enjoy living in God's world. And then we are better able to be His partners, to work with Him and help make the world better and better.

The minds and bodies that God gave us are very wonderful. If we use them wisely, we can enjoy ourselves and other people and the world. And it is right that we should!

In what we do to someone else
Our guide should always be:
Is this a thing that I would like
If he did this to me?

About two thousand years ago, a great and wise and gentle rabbi named Hillel explained one of the most important ideas in the Bible: "Love your neighbor as yourself." This means, he said, that you must not do things to other people that you would not want them to do to you. Another rabbi, Akiba, said that "Love your neighbor as yourself" is "The Great Rule" of the Bible.

Many, many religions have this same good rule. Jews have Hillel's rule. Christians have the Golden Rule. And other religions have the same kind of rule too.

This rule is also a kind of ruler, a measuring stick by which we can tell whether we are doing right or wrong. Do you want other people

to lie to you or steal from you?

to boast and brag?

Of course you don't. Then you must not lie to others or steal from them. You must not boast or brag or feel more important than other people.

Do you want other people
to be fair with you?
to be honest with you?
to be kind and friendly and helpful?
to share with you?
to remember that you are important?
to be sorry when they hurt you?
to forgive you when you hurt them?

Of course you do! Then you must be honest and fair with them. You must be kind and friendly and helpful to them. You must share with them and remember that they are important. You must be sorry when you hurt them, and forgive them when they hurt you. We should treat all other people the way we want them to treat us.

The rule of loving others as we love ourselves is a wise and good rule. It helps us choose between right and wrong. When we love our neighbors as ourselves, we are special. Then we really help make the world better. And then we really are God's partners.